Reimagining the Bazaars

Weaving Local Stories into Brands

TABISH KHAN

Made with ❤ on the Notion Press Platform

www.notionpress.com

To the Almighty.

Mamma , Pappa, Wahaj Bhai (My elder Brother) and Aapean (my late aunt) , for their endless love, belief, and support that have been the true foundation of everything I've achieved.

To my three wives Rehan, Waseem, and Ismail (my friends and Co-founders) for being my partners in crime, my pillars of strength, and my greatest collaborators. This journey wouldn't be the same without you all.

To my true mentor, Mr. Sanjay Kalyankar, whose thoughts and vision have profoundly shaped me, both knowingly and unknowingly.

To my first client, Vishal Nayak, thank you for believing in me when no one else did. To the countless brands I've crafted, each one is a reflection of my learning, my imagination, and my passion for bringing something new to life. This is for you—the dreamers, the doers, and the believers in a world where no idea is too small to make an impact.

This book is a tribute to the local markets and the people who inspire me to create, experiment, and dream. It's for those who dare to challenge the status quo, those who continuously evolve, and everyone who believes in the power of creativity to transform the world around them.

.

Contents

Foreword

It is with immense pride and joy that we pen this foreword for a book that is not merely a collection of ideas but a testament to the transformative power of creativity, vision, and determination. Tabish Khan, the author of Reimagining the Bazaar, is not just a colleague or a collaborator; he is a dear friend, a visionary, and a relentless innovator. Having shared the highs and lows of entrepreneurship with him, we, have witnessed firsthand his journey of reshaping the ordinary into the extraordinary.

This book holds within its pages a treasure trove of insights, not only for designers and entrepreneurs but for anyone who dares to dream of crafting something meaningful. It encapsulates Tabish's philosophy of blending tradition with innovation, logic with imagination, and the global with the local. Each chapter is a story in itself, offering lessons that resonate far beyond the realm of branding and design, speaking instead to the heart of anyone passionate about making an impact.

For us, this book is more than just a narrative; it is a masterclass in perseverance. Tabish's approach to reimagining local identities—whether through creating unforgettable brands or revolutionizing experiences—is nothing short of inspiring. His dedication to understanding the pulse of his audience and his ability to turn challenges into opportunities remind us why he is a force to be reckoned with in the world of creative innovation.

From late-night brainstorming sessions to the adrenaline-filled rush of launching campaigns, we've had the privilege of being part of this incredible journey. Every page of this book reflects the authenticity and passion that Tabish brings to his work, and we are confident that his insights will ignite a spark in readers, pushing them to think differently and challenge the status quo.

As you delve into Reimagining the Bazaar, you'll find yourself transported into a world where ideas meet execution, and tradition evolves into something timeless. Tabish, through his unparalleled storytelling and practical wisdom, will not just inspire you but compel you to take action.

This book is not just a reflection of the markets it celebrates—it is a reflection of the man behind it. And as his closest collaborators and friends, we couldn't be prouder to share this journey with you.

To the reader, we invite you to immerse yourself in this masterpiece and find your own path to reimagining the world around you. And to our friend, Tabish—thank you for continuing to inspire us and everyone around you.

With admiration and gratitude,

Waseem, Rehan and Ismail

Preface

When I first ventured into branding and design, I didn't anticipate how deeply it would intertwine with my identity. My name is Tabish Khan, and while I don't claim to be a genius or a perfect designer, I've approached this journey with relentless curiosity and a passion for learning. Over the years, I've had the privilege of collaborating with local markets, shaping brands that are more than products or services—they're vibrant reflections of the communities they come from.

Reimagining the Bazaars: Weaving Local Stories into Brands is not your traditional branding guide. It's not a collection of formulas or a showcase of polished perfection. Instead, it's a deeply personal account of my journey—one shaped by questions, experiments, and a willingness to embrace the imperfections of both the process and the markets I serve.

At its core, this book is an exploration of connection—how local stories and identities can be transformed into meaningful brands. Each project I've worked on has taught me valuable lessons, not just about branding but about the unique cultures and aspirations that define local markets.

Coming from a dual background—engineering by profession and branding by passion—I've learned to fuse logic with creativity and data with storytelling. This book reflects that blend, celebrating the uniqueness of every brand and the communities behind them.

Through these pages, you'll find not only insights and case studies but also my mistakes and moments of growth. From leading Aura Digital to co-founding projects with close friends, this journey has been as much about collaboration as it has been about self-discovery.

Whether you're a designer, entrepreneur, or someone intrigued by branding, I invite you to explore this book. Here, you'll find the stories of local clients and institutions, stories that honor the vibrant essence of bazaars and the people who breathe life into them.

Thank you for being part of this journey. I hope these pages inspire you to see branding not as a pursuit of perfection, but as a celebration of connection, creativity, and the human stories that shape our world.

Tabish Khan

Acknowledgments

Imaginations, dreams, manifestion and mistakes

Prologue

Branding, in its simplest form, isn't about logos or taglines—it's about connection. It's about understanding people—not just their needs, but their emotions, aspirations, and the cultures they live within. For me, branding is a journey, one filled with discovery, adaptation, and evolution.

This book is a personal portfolio—a collection of stories and insights from my experiences of working with local clients, businesses, and institutions. It's not a traditional guide to branding, but rather a look into the vibrant world of local bazaars and the challenges of transforming their unique stories into compelling brands.

I've always been fascinated by the energy of local markets. They're dynamic, diverse, and often overlooked by those trying to "globalize" them. Through trial and error, I've learned that branding isn't about perfection but about creating authentic connections. Each brand I've worked on reflects an attempt to capture the essence of its community, blending practicality with creativity and strategy with storytelling.

In this book, you'll find case studies of real projects— brands shaped by their local roots. From institutions to small businesses, each project has taught me that the power of branding lies in its ability to honor and amplify local identities.

This is a book about the people, challenges, and triumphs that have shaped my work. It's about crafting brands that resonate—not with a global audience, but with the communities that give them life. Welcome to "Reimagining the Bazaars: Weaving Local Stories into Brands"—where the local takes center stage, and every brand has a story worth telling.

Brewing Boldness The art and strategy behind Crunch N Quench

The Birth of a Vision

It all started with a simple idea—a cozy café that would blend premium vibes with affordability, appealing to the urban hustle of young professionals and students. Crunch N' Quench wasn't just a project; it was my dream, a canvas where I could blend creativity and strategy to craft something truly remarkable. From the logo to the menu, from the launch campaigns to the tiniest signage detail, every element of this café was a reflection of my design philosophy—minimal yet magnetic.

The idea brewed one evening while I was sipping coffee, sketching random ideas on paper. What if a café could feel like more than just a place to eat? What if it became a symbol of vibrant energy, a melting pot of ideas, or even a second home to its visitors? And that's where it clicked. The journey of Crunch N' Quench began.

Project Overview:
Crunch N' Quench is a semi-premium café brand specializing in mocktails and sandwiches. I developed its brand identity from scratch, blending traditional design principles with modern AI visuals.

Client Goal
To establish Crunch N' Quench as a go-to café for young professionals and students, offering a cozy yet premium experience through creative branding and marketing strategies.

Deliverables
Deliverables included brand identity development, strategic consulting, and execution across visual and digital touchpoints. This covered logo design, premium typography, signage, and cohesive social media assets to establish a consistent brand presence.

Research and Discussions
Based on our initial discussions, I was confident in pursuing a darker theme with metallic accents and a minimalist design. I conducted research on market trends, consumer psychology, and branding strategies to inform this direction. My goal was to create a project that is purely photo-oriented, embodying the concept of

"WHAT YOU SEE IS WHAT YOU GET."

Shaping the Brand Identity

Every detail of the café's identity carried meaning, inspired by the vibe I wanted the place to exude. The dark, stone-inspired interiors whispered sophistication, while the monochromatic black-and-white palette made it approachable. A hint of metallic accents sprinkled elegance without being intimidating.

Logo: A Symbol of Refreshment

Designing the logo felt like sculpting the café's soul. A sleek, stylized glass became the centerpiece, hinting at the café's expertise in beverages. Its vertical alignment wasn't just an aesthetic choice; it reflected adaptability, making it shine across formats—from Instagram posts to storefront signage.

Tagline: Mocktail Meets Munch

Crafting the tagline was one of the most exciting moments. It had to be punchy yet descriptive, encapsulating the café's essence. "Mocktail Meets Munch" wasn't just a line—it was a promise to customers looking for flavorful bites paired with refreshing drinks.

Brand Identity Development :

The logo was crafted to reflect the brand's essence, going beyond just the product. Centered around a fluid-filled glass and the name "Crunch n' Quench," the logo captures the refreshing, inviting nature of the café. Its design is versatile and scalable, adaptable across all mediums, from digital to physical signage. In line with my vision, the logo embodies a minimalistic, bold, and premium feel, setting the tone for a modern café experience that resonates with young, urban customers.

Making It Real: From Vision to Execution

The café's identity wasn't confined to design; it had to breathe life across touchpoints. This meant crafting experiences that would pull people in and make them stay.

Exterior Signage

I imagined the signage as a "welcome mat" for the brand—bold yet elegant. The metallic accents against a dark backdrop mirrored the café's interiors, while the clean, modern typeface whispered premium vibes.

Exterior Signage
Objective: Create an immediate impact and lasting impression.
Design: The signage combines metallic accents on a dark background to echo the café's interior ambiance, attracting passersby and enhancing brand recall.

Menu: The Silent Seller

Menus are often overlooked, but to me, they're a piece of storytelling. Using mouthwatering images and minimal layouts, I wanted every page to say, "Welcome to indulgence."

Menu Design

Objective: Reflect the café's premium positioning through clean layouts and high-quality visuals.

Design: The menu integrates rich, mouthwatering images and a minimalistic layout, aligned with the monochromatic theme, reinforcing the café's refined identity.

*Prices are not real

Instagram Grid: A Feast for the Eyes

Social media was our stage. I envisioned Crunch N' Quench's Instagram grid as an art gallery of its offerings. AI-generated visuals brought dishes to life, making every scroll an experience. The centerpiece? A logo reveal video that didn't just display the brand—it celebrated it.

AI driven Photography

I developed an Instagram grid designed to captivate viewers with a mix of AI-generated, high-dominance visuals featuring Crunch N' Quench's offerings. Each image was carefully curated to showcase the richness of the food and beverages, blending seamlessly into a cohesive feed.

Launch Day: The Moment of Truth

Launch day felt like an adrenaline rush. We kicked off with a cold coffee + cheese corn sandwich combo for 99, and the response was overwhelming. Seeing over 100 combos sell within hours was surreal.

Launch Offer

The launch offer for Crunch n' Quench featured an irresistible combo: Cold Coffee and a Cheese Corn Sandwich for just 99. This special deal was designed to attract first-time customers, allowing them to sample our signature items at an accessible price point. The promotion generated a buzz, bringing in over 100+ orders for combo during initial days and setting a lively tone for the café's debut.

Collaborating with local influencers proved to be a game-changer.we hit 72K views (with a limited budget) in no time. The buzz was electric, and the café's tables were buzzing with chatter and clinking glasses.

One of my favorite moments was seeing TEDx attendees enjoying their exclusive discounts. The café had become more than a place—it was now a part of meaningful conversations and events.

TEDx Sponsorship

TEDx Event Discounts: Offered exclusive discounts to TEDx attendees, positioning Crunch N' Quench as a thoughtful, premium choice.

Standees for Visibility: Placed branded standees around the college, highlighting popular combos and enhancing on-site brand presence.

Vouchers for Attendees: Gifted discount vouchers to guests, students, and volunteers, integrating Crunch N' Quench into the TEDx event experience.

Instagram Filter Campaign: Launched an interactive Q&A filter on Instagram, where participants with all

Lessons from the Crunch N' Quench Journey

Looking back, this journey wasn't just about launching a café; it was about learning the delicate art of storytelling through branding.

- Cohesion is Key: Whether it was the logo, menu, or Instagram grid, the consistent monochrome theme made the brand unforgettable.

- Emotion Matters: Speaking in the local language of visuals and content bridged a genuine connection with customers.

- Innovation Amplifies Impact: Leveraging AI-based visuals wasn't just trendy—it added a polished, futuristic feel to the brand.

Final Thoughts: A Dream Served Fresh

Crunch N' Quench taught me an invaluable lesson: branding is far more than just slapping logos onto merchandise or designing catchy visuals. It's about crafting a story—a compelling narrative that customers want to immerse themselves in, a story they want to tell as their own. It's about creating a connection, an identity, and a sense of belonging that goes beyond the product or service.

Watching people engage with the café has been an eye-opening experience. Seeing them tag their friends in photos, share their visits on social media, and make Crunch N' Quench a backdrop for their conversations and celebrations wasn't just fulfilling—it was profoundly personal. In those moments, the café wasn't just a place to grab a mocktail or sandwich; it became a part of their cherished memories, their unique stories. That connection transformed all the effort, from brainstorming to execution, into something truly meaningful.

Every evening, when I see the logo illuminated on the signage, I feel a deep sense of pride. It's a glowing reminder that every detail, every decision, and every late-night brainstorming session—no matter how small or tedious—played a role in creating something greater than the sum of its parts. Crunch N' Quench is more than a café; it's a testament to what happens when passion and purpose come together. It's a living, breathing example of how dreams, when nurtured with care and intent, can resonate far beyond their origin.

Key Results and Reflections

Brand Identity Recognition:
The visual identity was met with praise and high engagement on social media, attracting a core audience aligned with Crunch N' Quench's target market.

Customer Feedback:
Positive reactions to both in-café visuals and social media content reinforced the brand's positioning and indicated successful brand alignment with customer expectations.

Final Takeaways
This branding journey with Crunch N' Quench underscored the importance of a unified visual strategy across all platforms. The successful integration of AI-generated imagery with traditional branding elements, paired with a well-executed social media campaign, helped capture the attention of the target demographic. This case study demonstrates my capability to create an impactful, visually consistent brand presence that thrives both online and offline.

Thank you!
A heartfelt thank you to my client, Kshitij Kalyankar, for trusting me and providing the creative freedom needed to bring this vision to life. Your support made this project truly fulfilling, and I'm grateful for the opportunity to create something meaningful together.

*THANK YOU FOR READING
REGARDS, TABISH.K !*

MADE WITH LOVE , CHAI & SAMOSAS

The Birth of DeoTech: A Dream Turned Reality

This section is dedicated to the incredible volunteers of DeoTech and the unwavering support of Priyanka Ma'am, Manisha Ma'am, Poonam Ma'am, and Shah Sir.

It started with a question: How can we create a space where students don't just learn but thrive?

As a final-year engineering student at Deogiri Institute of Engineering and Management Studies, I often felt that something was missing in our academic environment—a platform where curiosity, creativity, and technology could come together. While lectures and labs taught us the basics, they left little room for experimentation, for diving headfirst into challenges that could spark true innovation.

At the same time there was an initiative by our dept to conduct an event that might be a second franchise of the earlier event that dept hosted , I was never to the support of this idea instead I forced lets get with a fresh identity a new vision a new aim a larger dream , created the identity in 1 night along with structure of committee and the future plan to my surprise the plan was accepted thanks to Priyanka maam, Manisha maam, Poonam maam , shah sir and our hod then Kalyankar sir

And so, DeoTech was born.

A Flagship Technical Fest Proudly Organized By
Deogiri Institute Of Engineering And Management Studies.

Which Aims To

Creating An Inclusive Platform For Students To Explore, Innovate, And Enjoy Technology, While Empowering Them With Analytical Skills And Entrepreneurship Abilities. Fostering A Dynamic Research Culture That Inspires Collaboration And Creativity, Making A Lasting Impact Within And Beyond The College Community.

I envisioned a flagship technical fest that wouldn't just be another event on the college calendar but a celebration of technology, creativity, and collaboration. A space where students could explore bold ideas, develop analytical skills, and experience the thrill of innovation. From this vision, DeoTech emerged as a platform to empower young minds, leaving a lasting mark both within the college and beyond its walls.

The Vision: Building Something Bigger

Creating DeoTech was about more than organizing a fest; it was about building a culture.

Purpose-Driven Beginnings

The idea for DeoTech came from observing a gap—a need for students to bridge the divide between what we learned in classrooms and the skills demanded by the real world. It was designed to prepare us for challenges we hadn't yet faced, blending curiosity with practical problem-solving.

The experiences I gained from attending some of the most vibrant and transformative cultural and tech fests across the country have been nothing short of extraordinary. Events like IIT Bombay's iconic Techfest, the dynamic cultural extravaganzas at IIM Bengaluru, and the grand showcases of innovation and creativity at renowned private universities left a profound impact on me.

These platforms were more than just events—they were ecosystems of ideas, collaboration, and boundless energy, where every moment was a testament to what can be achieved when talent meets opportunity. Witnessing the meticulous planning, the enthusiasm of the participants, and the sheer scale of these festivals sparked something within me.

They showed me the power of bringing people together under one shared vision, where creativity, technology, and culture converge to leave a lasting legacy. This inspiration has fueled my determination to channel that same level of passion and ambition into creating experiences that resonate deeply and make an impact.

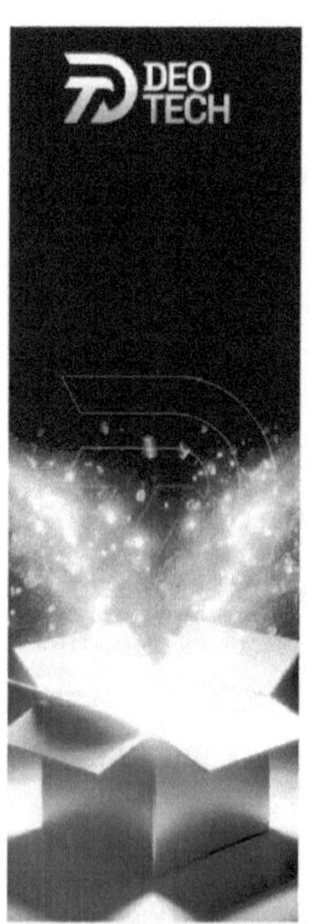

First Of All

we are grateful to our college for giving this **incredible opportunity to be the digital sponsor for this exciting event!**

The Need

DeoTech Is Needed To Provide Students With An inclusive Platform To Explore And Innovate With Technology, Empowering Them With Strong Analytical And Entrepreneurship Skills. It Fosters A Dynamic Research Culture, Encouraging Collaboration And Creativity Among Faculty And Students. Ultimately, DeoTech Aims To Make A Lasting Impact Within And Beyond The College Community.

Empowering Students

I wanted every student who walked into DeoTech to leave with more than just knowledge. Whether through coding challenges, workshops, or panel discussions, the event was a playground where students could learn by doing—where they could take risks, fail fast, and grow stronger.

Impact Beyond Campus

The dream wasn't confined to our college. DeoTech was built to ripple outward, sparking connections and ideas that could resonate in the wider tech community. My hope was for it to become a launchpad for innovation—a platform that would inspire students long after the event ended.

Bringing DeoTech to Life

Turning this vision into reality was a journey filled with late nights, countless iterations, and moments of doubt. But every challenge we faced only strengthened our resolve to make DeoTech something extraordinary.

Crafting the Identity

The first step was giving DeoTech a face—a brand identity that would reflect its bold and innovative spirit.

- The Name: "DeoTech" was a natural choice, blending the heritage of "Deogiri" with the universal appeal of "tech." It was simple, memorable, and deeply rooted in our college's identity.

- The Logo: The logo, a monogram of "D" and "T," was designed to be sleek and modern—just like the fest itself. It symbolized simplicity, focus, and forward-thinking.

- The Colors: Vibrant yet professional, the color palette balanced youthful energy with a premium feel, setting the tone for the event.

- Typography: Fonts like Space Grotesk and Satoshi brought a clean, contemporary edge to all the branding materials, ensuring clarity and sophistication.

Creating an Experience That Stood Out

Every aspect of DeoTech was designed to captivate and inspire, from the posters on campus to the digital campaigns on social media.

The Colours

the careful color selection ensures the event looks premium and exciting, effectively communicating with the youth for whom it is intended.

The Fonts

The Fonts Used Are Space Grotesk, Darker Grotesk, And Satoshi, Chosen For Their Clarity And Diverse Family Options.

The Feel

The Branding Has Been Designed To Appear Premium And Bold, Generating Excitement Among Students.

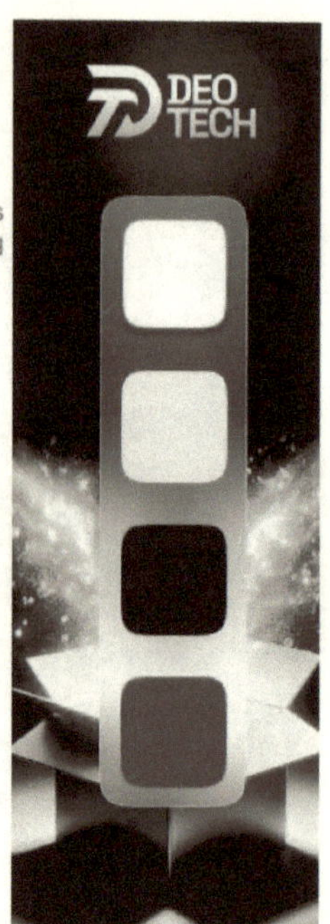

Bold Designs for Maximum Impact

The visual identity was striking—high-contrast designs that commanded attention. Whether it was a banner in the college foyer or a post on Instagram, everything about DeoTech screamed innovation and energy.

Seamless Communication

We knew the importance of keeping students informed and engaged. QR codes on posters provided instant access to event schedules and registration links, ensuring no one missed a thing.

Building a Connection Through Merchandise

Merchandise was more than a keepsake; it was a way for students to feel like they belonged.

Stickers and Badges: Designed with care, they became symbols of participation and pride. Seeing students proudly wear them felt like a win—it was proof that DeoTech had struck a chord.

A Collectible Series: The designs were bold and eye-catching, turning everyday items into cherished memories of the event.

Certificate Designs

The Website: Built for the Future

In just four hours, we built a website that captured the essence of DeoTech. The sleek, dark theme matched the fest's premium identity, while its user-friendly structure made it easy for students to navigate. It wasn't just for this year's event—it was a foundation bazould build on for years to come. A special thanks to my love Md.Rehan for crafting the website

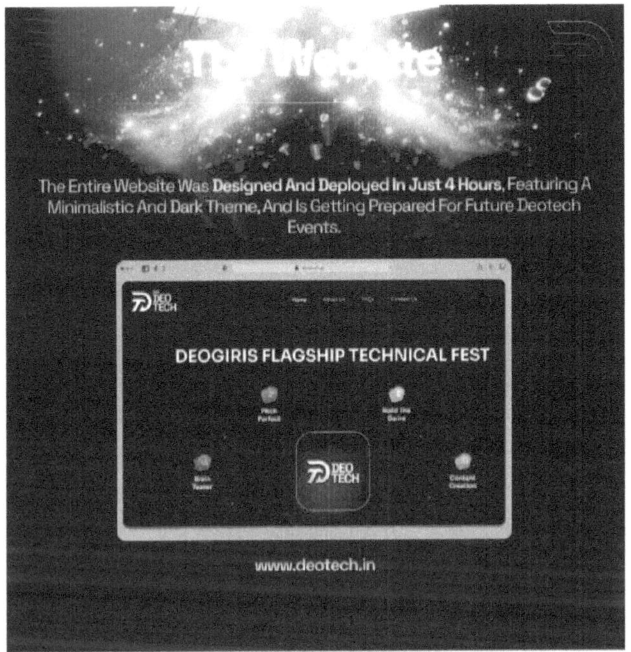

A Personal Milestone

For me, DeoTech was more than a project—it was a dream. And through Aura Digital, the creative agency I founded, I had the privilege of sponsoring the fest. It felt deeply personal, a full-circle moment where my passion for creativity and innovation found its perfect expression.

Looking Ahead

As I watched the students, coordinators, and volunteers come together to bring DeoTech to life, I felt a sense of pride that's hard to put into words. This wasn't just an event; it was the beginning of something bigger—a legacy that would continue to grow with every edition.

The success of DeoTech's first chapter has set the stage for what's to come. With every future event, I'm excited to see how this platform will continue to empower, inspire, and make an impact.

Special Thanks

DeoTech wouldn't have been possible without the unwavering support and guidance of some truly incredible individuals. I extend my heartfelt thanks to our then Head of Department, Mr. Sanjay Kalyakar, for believing in the vision of this fest. A special acknowledgment to our coordinators, Ms. Manisha Mundhe, Ms. Priyanka Dhas, Ms. Poonam Borase, and Mr. Sandeep Shah, whose dedication and hard work were instrumental in bringing DeoTech to life. Their encouragement and trust turned this dream into reality, and for that, I will always be grateful.

This Project Holds A Deeply Special Place In My Heart For Several Reasons. I Had Always Dreamed Of Seeing My Brand Name As One Of The Sponsors For A College Event. After Numerous Failed Attempts, Finally Getting This Opportunity Felt Surreal And Profoundly Meaningful. Doing Something For Our Own College Fills Me With Immense Pride And Joy.

I Am Profoundly Grateful To Each And Every Person Involved—The Coordinators, Volunteers, Organizing Committee, And, Of Course, The Participants. Your Dedication And Support Made This Dream A Reality. The Journey And The Legacy Have Just Begun, And I Am Incredibly Excited And Emotional About What The Future Of Deotech Holds. Thank You All For Being Part Of This Incredible Experience.

-Tabish Khan

Designing tradition The Namaste Branding Project

Introduction: A Journey of Empathy and Discovery

Branding is more than creating logos or defining color palettes; it's about understanding people, their emotions, and their values. When I took on the Namaste Branding project, I realized it was not just about designing a visual identity for a vegetarian restaurant chain—it was about stepping into the lives of a community that holds vegetarianism as a core belief.

To truly connect with this audience, I decided to embrace vegetarianism myself during the course of the project. This wasn't a symbolic gesture; it was an intentional step to better understand their emotions, values, and preferences. This immersive approach became the heart of my journey, shaping my design choices and deepening my empathy for the community.

Namaste Foods was envisioned as a group of restaurants catering to diverse vegetarian cuisines, with pav bhaji—a beloved Indian street food—as its signature offering. The client's vision was clear: create a brand that felt pure, welcoming, and culturally authentic. My challenge was to translate this vision into a design that resonated with the community, stood out in a competitive market, and became a symbol of trust and connection.

The First Steps: Discovering the Heart of Namaste Foods

My journey began with a series of in-depth conversations with the client. They shared their dreams and aspirations for Namaste Foods: a brand that would represent warmth, purity, and the richness of Indian tradition. These discussions revealed their desire for simplicity in design, coupled with a deep-rooted connection to cultural values.

I saw this project as an opportunity to go beyond aesthetics. My goal was to create an identity that wasn't just visually appealing but emotionally engaging—a brand that would make people feel at home while celebrating the essence of vegetarianism.

Exploration: Researching Culture and Cuisine

The next phase of the project involved extensive research into vegetarianism and its significance within Indian culture. I delved into its roots, understanding how vegetarianism is tied to purity, respect for life, and spiritual discipline.

I spent time interacting with families, students, and community members, gathering insights about their relationship with vegetarian food. These conversations were rich with stories about traditions, values, and the emotional connections people have with their meals. Each story added layers to my understanding, helping me craft a brand that would reflect these deep-seated values.

Designing the Namaste Identity

The Power of the Namaste Gesture, As I brainstormed ideas for the brand's identity, the "namaste" gesture emerged as a powerful symbol. A universal sign of respect and goodwill, the gesture embodies the essence of

Indian hospitality. It was the perfect representation of the warmth and inclusivity Namaste Foods aimed to offer.

I envisioned a logo that captured the simplicity and elegance of the namaste gesture. It wasn't just a design element—it was a reflection of the values that the brand stood for.

The Palette of Positivity

Colors play a vital role in shaping perceptions, and the choice of a color palette for Namaste Foods was a thoughtful process. The client's preference for green and yellow was rooted in their association with freshness, vitality, and positivity—qualities they wanted the brand to exude.

To create a modern yet grounded aesthetic, I introduced black as a complementary color. It provided contrast and clarity, ensuring the design was visually striking while staying true to its cultural roots.

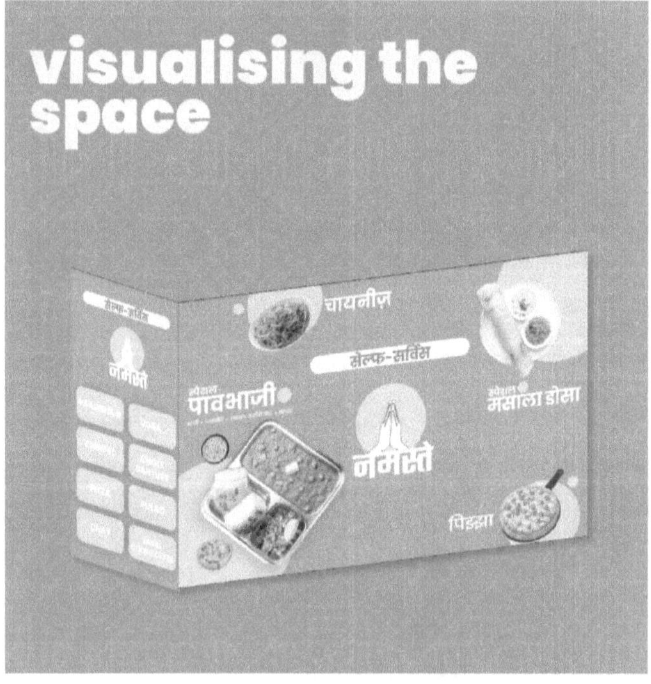

Crafting the Tagline: Words That Speak to the Soul

A tagline can often become the soul of a brand, encapsulating its mission and values in a few words. For Namaste Foods, I wanted a tagline that resonated deeply with the audience. After exploring various ideas, I landed on

"Aahar Shudho, Satvoshudhi" (Pure food, pure soul).

This tagline wasn't just a statement—it was a promise. It reflected the brand's commitment to purity and authenticity, while also celebrating the spiritual connection many have with vegetarianism.

Cultural Threads in Design: Beyond the Logo

Designing for Namaste Foods extended far beyond the logo. It involved crafting every element of the brand to reflect its cultural ethos:

- Staff Uniforms: Green polo shirts with yellow collars were designed to create a cohesive and professional look. The logo was prominently displayed, ensuring consistency across the brand.

- Signage and Standees: I created visually engaging signage that highlighted the restaurant's offerings. To connect with the local audience, Marathi was the primary language used, making the brand more relatable and accessible.

- Packaging and Collaterals: The designs were kept simple yet impactful, focusing on clean lines and the vibrant color palette to ensure they stood out.

Apparel design

The Emotional Reveal: A Promotional Video

The promotional video was a cornerstone of the branding strategy. It was designed to evoke a sense of nostalgia and pride. Traditional sounds, like the ringing of a temple bell, were paired with modern visuals to reveal the logo and introduce the brand to the audience.

This video wasn't just an announcement—it was an invitation for people to join a community that celebrated vegetarianism and Indian values.

The Grand Launch: A Celebration of Culture

- The launch of Namaste Foods was a moment of pride and excitement. We organized a grand opening event that included:

- Food Tastings: Guests sampled a variety of vegetarian dishes, experiencing the purity and richness of the cuisine.

- Cultural Performances: Traditional music and dance performances created an atmosphere of celebration and connection.

- Community Engagement: Activities like cooking demonstrations and story-sharing sessions helped establish a bond with the local audience.

The event was a resounding success, drawing families, students, and locals alike. However, it also revealed a critical oversight: the menu was primarily in English, which didn't resonate with the predominantly Marathi-speaking audience. This was a valuable learning experience, highlighting the importance of cultural alignment in every detail.

Key Takeaways: Lessons for the Future

- *Empathy Is Key: Immersing myself in the vegetarian lifestyle allowed me to design with authenticity and depth.*

- *Cultural Sensitivity Matters: From language to visuals, every element must reflect the audience's values and preferences.*

- *Adaptability Ensures Success: Addressing feedback and refining strategies post-launch is essential for growth.*

A Personal Journey of Growth

The Namaste Branding project was more than a professional endeavor—it was a deeply personal journey. It taught me the power of empathy, the importance of storytelling in design, and the impact of connecting with people on a cultural and emotional level.

Today, Namaste Foods stands as a symbol of purity and tradition, resonating with its audience and building lasting connections. For me, it's a reminder of why I chose this path: to tell stories, create meaning, and reimagine the bazaar, one brand at a time.

Through this project, I also discovered the profound influence of collaboration. Each idea, insight, and shared moment added layers of depth to the final outcome. Namaste Branding was not just about creating a visual identity—it was about weaving a shared vision into the fabric of the brand, making it not only memorable but truly timeless.

Heritage Unleashed
Creating a fusion food identity

Reimagining the Bazaar: The Story of Chaap Maharaj

In the heart of a bustling city, where food is not just a necessity but a way of life, there emerged a unique culinary vision—Chaap Maharaj. It wasn't just a place to eat; it was a cultural movement, an experience, and a celebration of vegetarian delights that few had ever truly explored before. And it all started with a simple yet powerful idea: Chaap—a beloved vegetarian delicacy—blended with the vibrant flavors of Chinese cuisine.

I remember the first time I met the founder of Chaap Maharaj. His excitement was palpable. The concept was clear: bring something new to the table—literally and figuratively. A fusion of traditional Chaap, a specialty in many Indian homes, and the beloved Chinese dishes that had become an integral part of the country's dining habits. But, as I listened to his story, it wasn't just about food. It was about bridging gaps between cultures, bringing people together, and offering them an experience unlike any other. The vision was set, and my role was to bring that vision to life.

The Genesis of Branding

Branding wasn't just about creating a logo or a color palette; it was about capturing the soul of Chaap Maharaj. It had to tell a story—a story that would resonate with the people, invoking feelings of warmth, nostalgia, and curiosity. The first step was crafting an identity that was unmistakably Chaap Maharaj.

I knew that the logo needed to reflect the fusion of culture and cuisine. It had to be bold yet traditional, modern yet rooted in the past. The idea of a moustache and a turban—symbols deeply embedded in Indian culture—was the cornerstone of our design. These elements would not only connect with the target audience but also honor the rich culinary heritage that the brand was built upon. The flowing typography of the word "Chaap" was an ode to the traditional attire, making sure that every curve and line evoked a sense of locality and familiarity. It wasn't just a logo; it was a visual conversation with the customers, speaking to their hearts.

But the logo alone wasn't enough. We needed characters, mascots, that would add playfulness to the brand and engage customers in a meaningful way. These mascots became more than just illustrations; they were part of the storytelling, inviting everyone into the world of Chaap Maharaj.

The Colors and the Space

The next task was to design the space—both the kiosk and the shop—that would house the spirit of Chaap Maharaj. We needed an environment that would transport customers into a world where vibrant colors and engaging design met the scent of freshly cooked food. For the kiosk, we wanted something that would stop people in their tracks. It had to be bold, eye-catching, and inviting. We used bright colors—lively greens, warm oranges, and deep reds—reflecting the vibrant nature of the food and the warmth of vegetarian dining. Every corner, every detail was carefully crafted to catch the eye, but also to foster curiosity.

The Colors and the Space

The shop layout was just as important. We wanted to create a space where people felt at home, a place where they could sit back, relax, and savor the experience. Comfortable seating, cozy decor, and thematic elements that spoke to the brand's lively spirit made the space more than just a dining area. It became an extension of the story we were telling.

VISUALISING THE
SPACE
CHAAP MAHARAJ
CHAAPS
TIKKA'S
ROLLS
CHINESE
SOYA CHAAP
PANEER TIKKA
CHAAP MAHARAJ
DELHI CHAAP N' DESI CHINESE
ROLLS
CHINESE
CHAAP MAHARAJ
SOYA CHAAP
CHINESE
PANEER TIKKA

The Menu: A Visual Feast

The menu was not just a list of items—it was part of the visual experience. With high-quality images of Chaap and Chinese dishes, the menu invited customers into a world of delicious possibilities. It wasn't enough to simply list the items; we wanted them to see the food, to imagine the tastes, to salivate over the choices before them. Every section of the menu was meticulously designed to be easy to navigate and filled with enticing visuals that made you want to try everything. The vegetarian focus was clear, reinforcing the brand's commitment to health-conscious dining without compromising on flavor.

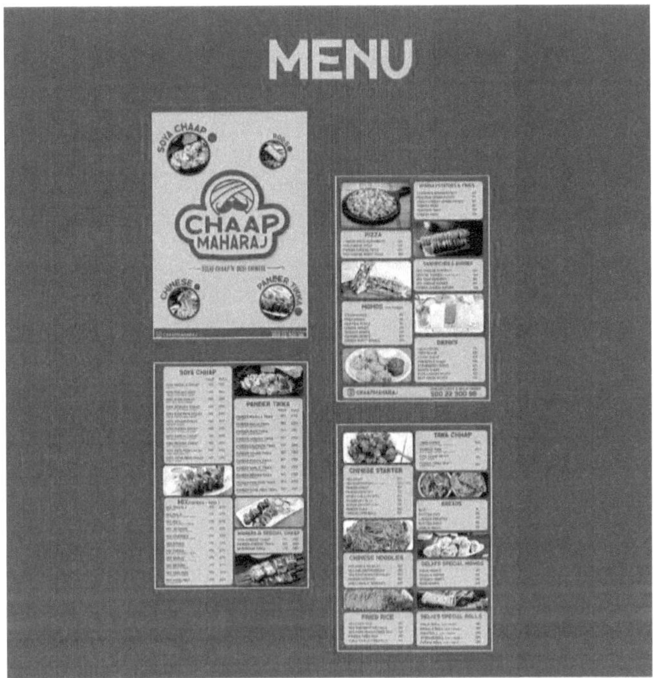

The Uniform: Professionalism with a Personal Touch

Staff uniforms might seem like a small detail, but they played an important role in ensuring that the Chaap Maharaj experience was cohesive. The polo t-shirts, aprons, and caps all featured the bold logo, ensuring that staff were not only easy to recognize but also that they represented the brand with professionalism. They weren't just servers; they were ambassadors of the brand, delivering an experience as memorable as the food itself.

Social Media: A Digital Connection

Branding doesn't end at the door of the physical space; it extends into the digital world. I worked closely with the team to create an Instagram grid strategy that would bring the same energy to social media as we had in the shop. Each post was designed with care—vibrant images, behind-the-scenes shots, and posts that shared the cultural significance of Chaap. The goal was to create a visual narrative that would engage followers and create a connection between the online experience and the physical space.

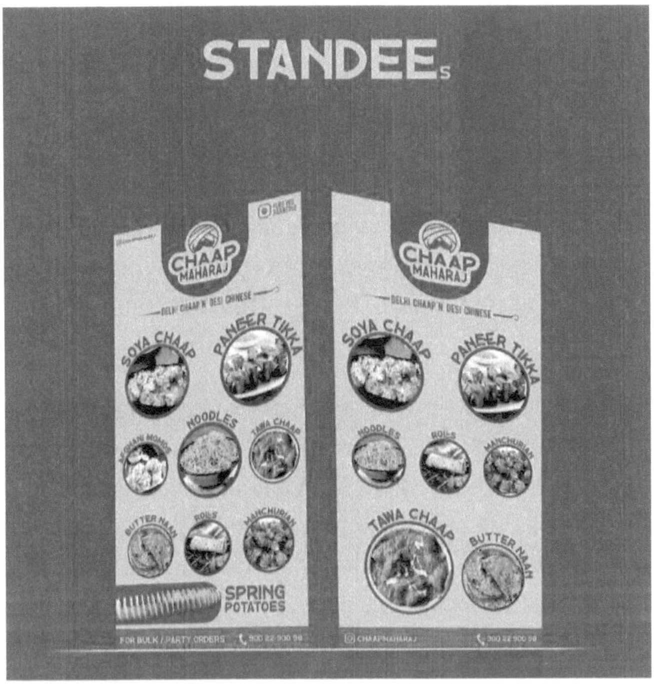

In the shop, the Instagram posts came to life through framed prints of the same designs. The experience didn't just end when you left the restaurant; it followed you home, seamlessly bridging the gap between the digital and physical worlds. This connection created a sense of belonging, encouraging customers to share their experiences and become part of the Chaap Maharaj community.

A Journey, Not Just a Meal

As Chaap Maharaj opened its doors, it became more than just a restaurant. It became a place where people gathered, where stories were shared over plates of delicious food, and where the brand's vibrant identity connected with customers on a deeper level. It was a place where culture, food, and design came together to create an unforgettable experience.

Through the power of branding, we didn't just build a business—we built a community. The story of Chaap Maharaj is not just one of food and design; it's a story of connection, of reimagining the bazaar, and of creating something truly meaningful for the local community. And this is just the beginning.

Crafting IBS A Regal Identity for Shawarma

The Story of Irani Bros Shawarma's Transformation

In the bustling heart of the city, where the air hums with the sounds of street vendors and quick bites, a new contender was about to change the way people thought about shawarmas. But not just any shawarma – this was to be an experience. An experience that felt as luxurious as it tasted. The task was clear: to create a brand identity that was not just about food, but about an elevated experience, one that combined royal aesthetics with the authentic flavors of the Middle East.

This was the challenge presented by Irani Bros Shawarma (IBS), a new venture with big dreams and the ambition to redefine what quick-service dining could be. IBS wasn't content with being another shawarma joint in the ever-crowded market. They wanted more – they wanted to bring a premium feel to a dish that was traditionally humble. And it was my job to make that happen.

The Vision: A Royal Revolution

IBS's founders envisioned a brand that blended authentic Middle Eastern flavors with luxury, offering more than just food, but an immersive dining experience. Their mission was clear – to elevate the shawarma experience with high-quality ingredients, sophisticated flavors, and a touch of royalty that felt both modern and inviting. The vision wasn't just about feeding people – it was about making them feel special with every bite.

BRIEF:

Create a Brand, Should look Royal, Premium!

The goal was to create a space where millennials and Gen Z, with their passion for bold flavors and unique dining experiences, could indulge in something that felt both indulgent and refined. And for families, a place that was welcoming, offering comfort without sacrificing quality.

The Challenge: Limited Time, Unlimited Potential

The road to rebranding was not easy. With tight budget constraints and a short timeline, the team needed a creative solution to achieve a luxurious feel on a limited scale. The typical route of professional photoshoots and high-end marketing tactics would be far too expensive and time-consuming. We had to think outside the box – we needed a strategy that could deliver sophistication and grandeur without stretching the budget too thin, AI was for the rescue again.

The Creative Spark: Luxury Through Simplicity

To meet these constraints, I turned to AI-generated visuals as a tool to quickly create stunning imagery that could elevate the brand's presence without the hefty price tag. Platforms like MidJourney allowed us to craft sophisticated, high-impact visuals in record time, giving us the polished, high-end look we were after. The result was a luxurious aesthetic achieved with minimal resources – a true example of creativity and technology coming together to defy expectations.

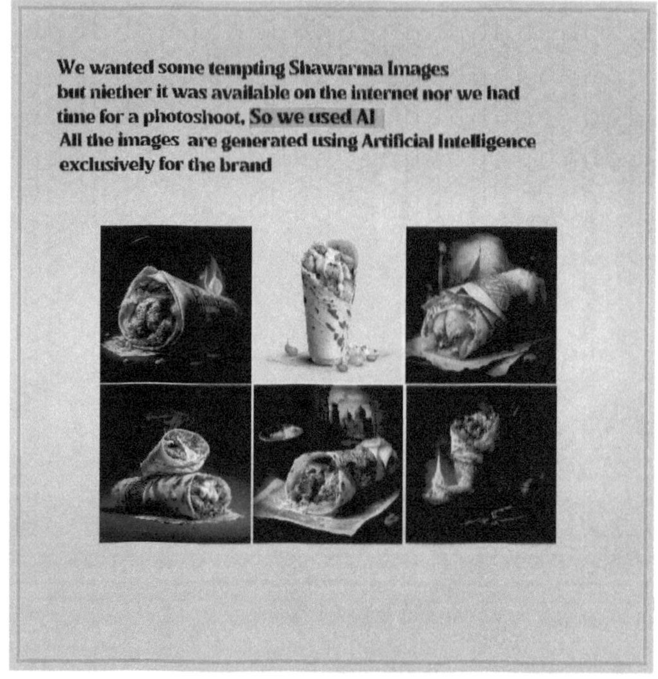

The Brand Identity: A Fusion of Old and New

From the very beginning, the identity of IBS had to feel royal yet approachable. Navy blue and gold became our signature colors. Navy, symbolizing trust and sophistication, and gold, representing wealth and quality. These colors spoke to the heart of the brand's message: that IBS was more than just a meal; it was an experience. The gold shawarma skewer icon, placed boldly against the deep blue background, became an emblem of authenticity and luxury. It wasn't just a logo; it was a symbol of the brand's promise to deliver both authenticity and refinement in every bite.

The menu also reflected this luxurious approach. The star dishes – fried chicken, exotic salads, and falafel – were designed to cater to the diverse tastes of the target audience. Each ingredient was carefully chosen for its quality, with fresh vegetables in the salads, hearty fried chicken, and authentic falafel adding layers of flavor to an already stellar offering.

Creating a Connection: A New Kind of Experience

Understanding that the younger audience engaged with brands not just through products but through experiences, we designed an interactive Instagram filter that invited customers to become part of the story. The filter allowed users to "virtually" order and interact with the brand online, creating a buzz and encouraging user-generated content. This simple tool helped spread the message about IBS in an organic, fun way, allowing customers to share their excitement and contribute to the growing brand presence.

Crafted
a Fun ordering
Exprience at
IBS

Thanks Waseem for being the face of this filter

The Launch: A Moment of Anticipation

The next step was to build anticipation. To do this, I created a campaign titled #IBSLaunch, with the tagline, "Authentic Shawarmas Coming Soon…". The campaign wasn't just about selling food – it was about building excitement for the premium, one-of-a-kind dining experience that IBS promised. Through exclusive offers like "Buy 2 Get 1 Free", we encouraged group dining, allowing the brand to attract larger groups while also emphasizing value.

Though the strategy didn't work as we were not able to handle the crowd, Every idea that seems to be good is not always practical to do

Influencer Magic: Spreading the Word

The influencer collaborations played a crucial role in spreading the word. I partnered with local food bloggers and micro-influencers who had a strong following in the city's food scene. Their exclusive sneak peeks into IBS's menu and ambiance helped create an aura of exclusivity and buzz around the brand before its official launch. These influencers didn't just post about IBS – they shared the experience, creating genuine, word-of-mouth excitement.

Results: A Royal Success

When IBS opened its doors, it wasn't just another shawarma spot. It was a phenomenon. The visual identity, with its deep navy and gold palette, resonated with customers on an emotional level. The blend of royal elegance with a modern, accessible twist spoke to the aspirations of its young, urban audience, and the offerings – fried chicken, exotic salads, and falafel – were unlike anything else in the market.

Despite the limited resources, IBS succeeded in establishing itself as a premium shawarma destination from day one. The AI-driven designs saved us time and money, delivering a polished look while maintaining the brand's upscale appeal. The use of market research to curate four signature combos and the introduction of enticing promotions like "Buy 2 Get 1 Free" brought in customers who returned not just for the food but for the experience.

By the end of the first month, IBS had firmly positioned itself as a go-to premium QSR destination in the city. Word-of-mouth buzz, bolstered by the influencer collaborations and social media activity, created a ripple effect that ensured the brand's presence was felt far beyond its physical location.

Reflecting on the Journey

When I look back at the IBS project, I see it as more than just a branding exercise. It was a lesson in creativity, innovation, and resourcefulness. In the face of constraints, we managed to craft something that was both luxurious and accessible, a reflection of the bazad's commitment to quality and the community's hunger for something new. IBS's success was not just in its visual identity or menu, but in the way it made people feel – special, valued, and part of something bigger.

Through this journey, I learned that the best brands are built not just on products, but on emotional connections. And with IBS, we did just that – we reimagined the humble shawarma and elevated it into an experience that was worthy of royalty.

Thanks , Learning , Conclusions & Outcomes

Learning: The Irani Bros Shawarma project underscored the significance of crafting a compelling brand identity that blends traditional and modern elements to attract a diverse audience. It highlighted the effective use of technology, such as AI-generated visuals, to create high-quality branding on a budget. Additionally, understanding consumer preferences—particularly among Millennials and families—was crucial for developing engaging promotions and interactive marketing strategies.

Conclusion: The project successfully established IBS as a premium shawarma brand, redefining the quick service restaurant experience. By focusing on high-quality offerings and an inviting atmosphere, IBS not only differentiated itself in a crowded market but also set new standards for shawarma dining. The strategic approach to branding and marketing laid a solid foundation for long-term success.

Outcomes:

Established a premium brand identity that appeals to target audiences.
Increased brand awareness through a successful launch campaign, generating buzz and initial foot traffic.
Engaging promotions, such as the "Buy 2 Get 1 Free" offer, encouraged group dining experiences.

Designing Cravings The Moh Maya Momos Brand Evolution

Project Context for MMM (Moh Maya Momos)

When I first sat down with the founder of Moh Maya Momos (MMM), the vision was clear but ambitious—transform the humble momo into a professional, approachable, and scalable food experience. This wasn't just about branding; it was about reimagining the way we look at momos in the fast-food industry.

The Brief

The founder envisioned a logo that not only captured the essence of momos but also looked professional with a touch of premium appeal. The challenge? Incorporating a real image of momos while still communicating a high-end feel. It needed to be bold, clear, and instantly recognizable. But that was just the beginning—MMM wanted to highlight its USP: three signature dips that would elevate the momo-eating experience.

The Ask:

The founder also requested packaging that wasn't just functional but that would interact with the customer, bringing a sense of excitement and connection. And above all, the packaging had to stand out in a crowded marketplace where competitors lacked any strong visual identity. This was the perfect opportunity to define a brand from the ground up, creating something special for a growing and competitive QSR market.

Brand Overview:

MMM—short for Moh Maya Momos—sets itself apart from the competition with a unique offering of flavorful momos served with three signature dips. Their menu is full of variety, keeping things fresh, affordable, and packed with taste. This wasn't just a food brand; it was a concept designed to provide a holistic and delicious experience.

Mission:

MMM's mission is nothing short of transformational. Just like KFC revolutionized fried chicken, MMM is set to professionalize the momo industry. They aim to create a chefless, scalable business model, with a medium-range franchise system. This vision will allow MMM to grow rapidly, expanding across India and setting a new standard for quality and consistency in the fast-food sector.

Target Audience:

MMM's primary focus is on Gen Z and early millennials—the food-loving, adventurous crowd who seek bold, affordable flavors. But it also appeals to momo lovers of all ages, bringing a wide spectrum of customers together under one roof.

The Branding Need:

In a city filled with local momo vendors, MMM saw an untapped opportunity. Most of the vendors operated without any strong branding, offering no real identity or sense of professionalism. The competition was fierce, but no one was standing out.

Brief's

The founder wanted the logo in such a way that it should contain a real image of momos

The logo should look professional and should posses a slight feel of Premiumness

He wanted to highlight the three dips concept that the brand is providing to the consumers

The brand uses two types of pacaking, we were asked to design the packaging in such a way that it should be bold and clear, and also should interact with the customers

MMM's solution was simple: build a brand that speaks to its target audience. The goal was to create a compelling identity that would resonate deeply with customers, positioning MMM as not just a momo joint, but the go-to momo destination. The need for brand development, identity, and structure became clear.

Market Research Insights:

To understand how we could make MMM stand out, we dove deep into the market and uncovered a range of opportunities and challenges:

- Limited Average Order Value (AOV): With small portions and limited menu options, local vendors had reached the cap of what a customer could spend.

- Time Restrictions: Most momos were only available after 4 PM, which hindered sales during the day.

- Branding and Packaging Gaps: Local vendors lacked any real brand identity. Their packaging was basic, and there was no effort to communicate quality or professionalism.

- Operational Issues: Many vendors were stuck in the chef-dependent model, limiting scalability and consistency.

- Poor Integration with Delivery Platforms: Few vendors were present on delivery apps, missing out on the growing demand for convenience.

- Strengths of Current Vendors: Despite these issues, local vendors did have a few strong points:

- Taste & Quantity: The generous portions and flavor were what kept customers loyal.

The Strategic Roadmap:

Armed with these insights, it was clear that MMM had a unique opportunity to carve out a niche in the market. The strategy focused on differentiation, scalability, and most importantly, professionalism.

Brand Positioning:

MMM was to be positioned as a tasteful, affordable, yet professional food option, similar to the transformation that KFC brought to fried chicken. The brand would be fun and approachable, yet still high-quality, offering something that could cater to the younger generation while appealing to older momo lovers as well.

Key Brand Pillars:

- A chefless model that would allow MMM to grow rapidly without sacrificing quality.

- A franchise system that would empower others to carry the MMM brand across India.

- Prioritize flavor while keeping the pricing accessible for Gen Z and millennials.

- Three signature dips to enhance the momo experience, adding variety and unique flavor.

- Opening kiosks at 12 PM to capture lunch crowds, extending hours beyond the typical post-4 PM rush.

- Improve efficiency to reduce wait times and speed up service, particularly for delivery platforms.

- A vibrant, engaging brand identity that appeals to younger, tech-savvy customers.

- Mini Moh, the brand's mascot, embodies this fun, youthful spirit and helps to connect emotionally with the target audience.

Creative Development for MMM

Brand Personality:

The goal was clear: create a brand that felt fun, vibrant, and youthful—something that could speak to the heart of Gen Z while maintaining a professional feel. We landed on the idea of a mascot—Mini Moh—a charming little momo character. Mini Moh quickly became the embodiment of the brand: playful, fun, and filled with personality. He became more than just a logo; he was MMM's spokesperson, symbolizing everything the brand stood for.

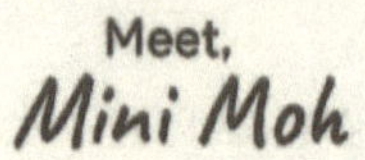

Color Palette: To stand out in a competitive space, we chose colors that would evoke energy, joy, and a touch of sophistication: Yellow for enthusiasm, youthfulness, and vibrancy. Purple to add depth, luxury, and a sense of wisdom.

Together, these colors set the stage for a bold yet approachable brand identity.

Typography

We selected the Anja Font, which had soft, inviting curves. It reinforced the friendly, approachable nature of MMM while staying modern and relevant.

Final Logo and Tagline:

The final logo is a perfect blend of playful and professional. Mini Moh was placed at the center, surrounded by bright colors and fun typography. The logo was responsive, meaning it would look great across any platform, from food trucks to delivery bags.

Tagline:

"Stuff With Goodness" became the mantra for the brand, emphasizing both the quality and the wholesome experience of enjoying MMM's delicious momos.

Implementation and Execution

With the branding finalized, the next step was ensuring the logo and design elements were applied consistently across all touchpoints.

Brand Application:

- From food trucks to kiosks and restaurants, the identity worked across different formats. The mascot, color scheme, and playful typography remained consistent, whether seen on a large truck or a small food container.

- Scalability was key. The design had to maintain its visual impact, whether displayed on a giant billboard or a small digital icon.

Packaging Design:

The packaging was more than just functional—it was an experience. With bright colors, quirky messages, and interactive elements, it brought the brand to life, making each order feel personal and memorable. Mini Moh was front and center, creating a deep emotional connection with customers.

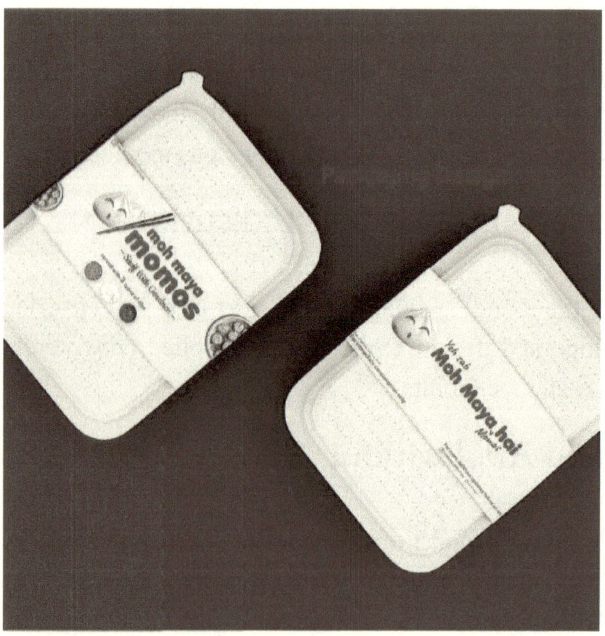

Digital Presence and Delivery Platforms:

MMM's branding also extended to the digital realm, with its identity seamlessly integrated into platforms like Zomato and Swiggy. The bright color scheme and fun visuals stood out in crowded app spaces. Social media campaigns featured Mini Moh, bringing an extra layer of engagement and playfulness to the brand's online presence.

Our Process/Aura Spice

Over a detailed discussion with the founder we understood the briefs for the brand

We wanted to create a mascot for the brand that should eventually become the face of the brand

For this purpose we created the *Mini Moh* 

We designed the packaging in such a way that it should comunicate with the consumers and should add a smile on their faces

Conclusion: Reimagining the Momo Industry

With this complete branding overhaul, MMM is positioned to revolutionize the momo industry. It's more than just a fast-food chain—it's a brand that resonates with its target audience, builds emotional connections, and stands out in a crowded market. By blending professionalism with fun, MMM has set itself up for long-term success, with plans for nationwide franchise expansion already in the works. And so, this small momo shop is now ready to take on the world—one delicious bite at a time.

Reimagining Dynamite Wrap & Rolls A Branding Journey

Reimagining Dynamite Wrap & Rolls: A Branding Journey

When I first encountered Dynamite Wrap & Rolls, a small but ambitious quick-service food brand, they were ready to make some noise in the market. The challenge? To create a packaging design that would not only reflect their energetic and playful personality but also stand out in the crowded world of quick bites. It wasn't just about wrapping food; it was about wrapping up an experience— one that would speak to young, hungry food lovers who crave not only flavor but also fun.

The Beginning: Understanding the Essence

I began by diving deep into market research, studying competitors and understanding consumer behavior. Quick-service food packaging isn't just functional; it's a marketing tool, a visual conversation with the customer. I wanted to make sure we were speaking the right language. Through the research, I discovered that Dynamite Wrap & Rolls had something unique—they didn't just want to sell food; they wanted to sell an experience that combined convenience with joy. And that's when it hit me: the packaging needed to embody that playful energy.

Crafting the Visual Identity

The next step was to craft a visual identity that truly reflected the brand's spirit. I knew that red was the key. It's bold, it's energetic, and it gets your attention. But more than that, red is scientifically proven to stimulate appetite—a perfect match for a food brand. The packaging design became a vibrant canvas, with the bold red background drawing you in, while a crisp white font stood out to highlight key phrases like "WRAP OR A ROLL." The typography was chosen not just for its readability but for its boldness—everything had to be loud, proud, and unapologetically fun. It was a playful jab at the seriousness of traditional food packaging, inviting the customer into a world of flavor and fun.

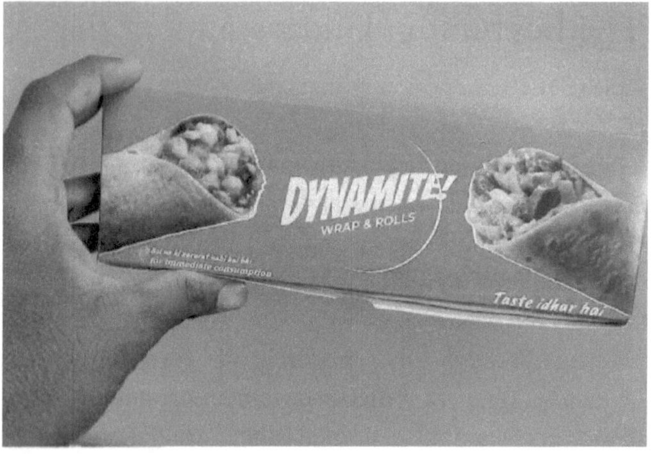

At both ends of the packaging, images of the wraps teased the product itself, giving the consumer a glimpse into the deliciousness inside. It was visual storytelling—no surprises, just a promise of a great meal.

And then there was the logo—Dynamite. Positioned dead center, it ensured that no matter where you were in the journey of unwrapping the product, you couldn't miss the brand. The logo wasn't just a design—it was a statement of identity.

The Magic of Words

Branding isn't just about colors and shapes; it's about the words we use. The copy had to match the playfulness of the design, and I wanted it to speak directly to the heart of the consumer. So, we introduced a little humor with phrases like, "Rules for eating a wrap or a roll — Ignore the above statement." It wasn't just a message; it was a conversation. It made the consumer smile before they even took their first bite.

But humor wasn't the only tool in our arsenal. We wanted the brand to feel local, to feel like it belonged. So, we included the phrase, "Yeh Wrap Hai Rapachick!"—a playful local twist that connected the brand with the cultural context of its audience. It wasn't just about selling food; it was about creating an emotional connection with the people it served.

We also made sure to include clear calls to action. "Order Online," with the familiar Swiggy and Zomato logos, made it easy for customers to think beyond the moment of consumption. The goal wasn't just to get them to buy once; we wanted to keep them coming back for more. We even threw in a little urgency with, "For immediate consumption only," reminding customers that the wrap was as fresh as it was fun.

The Practical Side of Things

Packaging might be a work of art, but it's also a work of practicality. For a quick-service food brand, the material had to be as functional as it was aesthetic. The wraps needed to stay fresh and warm, and the material had to be easy to handle and dispose of. This wasn't just about looking good on the shelf—it was about the experience from start to finish.

The rectangular layout made the packaging easy to grab and go. With well-spaced information, there was no confusion for the customer, ensuring a smooth, streamlined experience every time.

Yeh wrap hai Raapchick!

Who Was This For?

This design wasn't for just anyone—it was crafted with a very specific audience in mind. Young adults, food enthusiasts, and those who value convenience, culture, and a little bit of humor. These are the people who are looking for a meal that's more than just food; they're after an experience, something to enjoy and talk about.

The bold colors, the cheeky language, and the overall fun vibe all spoke directly to this demographic—those who crave not just a meal, but a memorable moment.

Standing Out in the Crowd

What made Dynamite Wrap & Rolls stand out wasn't just the flavor of the food; it was the personality that the brand exuded. The playful, quirky tone of the packaging set it apart from more generic fast-food brands.And the unique selling proposition (USP)? It wasn't just about being another wrap in the market—it was about providing an experience that would stick in your mind. The humor, the local touch, and the bold design made the brand not just something you ate but something you remembered.

Wrapping It Up

When it all came together—the vibrant colors, the witty messaging, the cultural relevance—it was clear: the Dynamite Wrap & Rolls packaging was more than just functional. It was an extension of the brand's identity. The humor, the boldness, and the practicality all worked together to create an experience that delighted and engaged customers, from the moment they saw the packaging to the moment they took that first bite.

This project was a perfect example of how packaging can go beyond its functional purpose to become a key part of the brand experience. It wasn't just about the wrap inside—it was about the story we told, the connection we made, and the joy we created. And for Dynamite Wrap & Rolls, it was only the beginning.

8. Redesigning for Revenue 114% AOV Boost at MMM

Reimagining Dynamite Wrap & Rolls: A Branding Journey

At Moh Maya Momos (MMM), my goal was clear: identify the factors limiting the Average Order Value (AOV) and implement strategies to overcome them, ultimately increasing revenue. To do this, I started by immersing myself in the customer experience, observing their journey from the moment they browsed the menu to the moment they placed their orders. What I discovered was a key insight: customers were hesitant. They lingered, unsure of what to order, and their uncertainty led them to make conservative, lower-value choices. As a result, AOV remained low.

Through a deeper analysis, it became clear that the root cause of this hesitation was the menu itself. The design was a barrier to confident decision-making. I pinpointed several issues:

- Lack of Visual Appeal: The menu was packed with text and lacked images, making it difficult for customers to picture their meals. Without visual cues, the ordering process felt overwhelming, prompting them to stick to familiar, low-cost options.

- Too Much Variety, No Focus: The menu offered an extensive list of items across multiple categories, with no clear emphasis on higher-value dishes. This created a sense of decision fatigue, causing customers to opt for simpler, cheaper options.

- Unstructured Layout: The menu's lack of clear organization made it hard to navigate. Customers struggled to differentiate between categories, understand pricing, or locate specialty items, which contributed to a chaotic ordering experience.

Recognizing these barriers, I knew I needed to redesign the menu. The goal was to make the menu more intuitive, visually appealing, and strategically curated to encourage higher-value orders.

THE OBSERVATION

After spending good amount of time in the restaurant we observed the AOV(Average order value) of the customer was limited because of the **weird ordering experience!**

THE PROBLEM

The problem we noticed was with the ***menu card*** , as it was kind of *visually unclear*

swipe

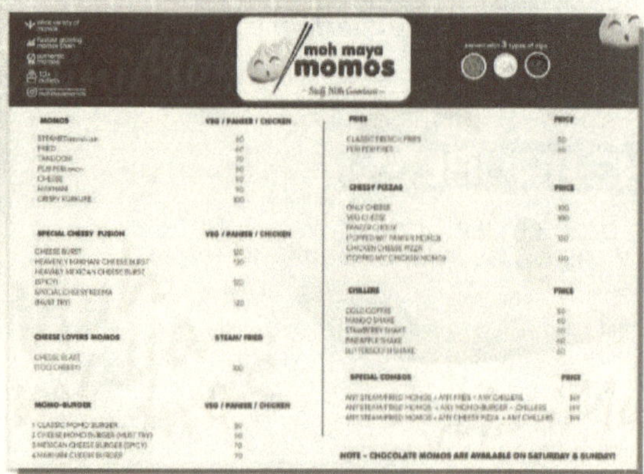

The Menu Redesign: A New Approach

I began by streamlining the menu. I reduced the number of items to minimize decision fatigue, allowing customers to focus on a select few options. I curated the menu to highlight high-value dishes that could help drive up AOV.

I then incorporated high-quality images for each item. This visual connection allowed customers to better imagine what they were ordering, fostering trust and sparking interest in premium dishes. Images bridged the gap between expectation and reality, encouraging customers to try something new.Next, I restructured the layout to create clear sections and a logical flow. Each item now had a name, price, and image, making it easier for customers to browse and compare. I strategically placed premium items in prominent locations, subtly guiding customers toward higher-value choices.

Drawing inspiration from food delivery apps, I applied a digital-inspired design to the physical menu. This familiar interface made browsing feel intuitive and modern. I also positioned high-margin items at eye level to further enhance the experience.

THE SOLUTION

We suggested to **decrease** the number of products in the menu and **redesigned** the menu!

We believe in the fact that it totally depends on the restaurant what they want to get ordered from the consumers

swipe

Immediate Results: A Transformative Effect

The impact of the new design was immediate. Customers responded positively, leading to a staggering 114% increase in AOV. The clearer, more engaging menu gave customers the confidence to explore higher-value items, resulting in larger orders. With a more intuitive layout and visual cues, the ordering process felt easier and more enjoyable, encouraging customers to try new items.

This redesign not only boosted revenue but also improved customer satisfaction. Customers were more confident in their choices, creating a more satisfying dining experience. This shift likely contributed to higher retention and repeat visits. By strategically curating the menu and focusing on key dishes, I was able to guide customers toward choices that were both more profitable for the business and more exciting for the diners.

NEW MENU

The new menu was a **Hit instantly** , we could see the **increase** in the avg order value and we clearly knew the reason for it!

Reducing the number of items significantly was a risky choice , however it gave us the freedom to highlight the stuff that we want the consumer to order

Associating image with every item played an important role, the consumer felt more connected as they knew exactly which product they'll be getting while ordering

Highlighting the price & the name we made distinct blocks for each items , with their subcategories, name & the price

Merging online & offline we took inspiration from the User interfaces in the food delivery apps & simply applied to the offline world

swipe

Key Insights: What I Learned

This project taught me several valuable lessons about the role of design in the customer experience:

- Understanding Customer Behavior: By observing customer hesitation, I was able to design a solution that directly addressed their needs, leading to a more confident and satisfying dining experience.

- The Power of Visuals: Adding images helped customers better envision their meal, bridging the gap between expectation and reality and encouraging them to order more.

- Streamlining for Strategic Influence: A well-curated menu can subtly guide customers toward choices that benefit both the restaurant and the diners, enhancing the overall experience.

- Adapting Digital Design to Physical Spaces: The familiarity of digital menu design principles worked effectively in a physical space, providing a modern, intuitive browsing experience that customers appreciated.

& THIS IS HOW

small changes made a big difference for us & the client

It happened because we knew the targeted audience & their behaviour, we observed the problem and the solution lead us to this remarkable result!

Conclusion: A Design-Driven Success

In the end, the redesign of the menu not only transformed the ordering experience but also resulted in a significant 114% increase in AOV. This project underscored the power of design in influencing customer behavior and enhancing the dining experience. It proved that when design is thoughtful and strategic, it can drive revenue, improve customer satisfaction, and ultimately transform a business. This success story serves as a testament to the importance of design in reimagining the bazaar—whether physical or digital.

CCC College Campaign

The Successful CCC Campaign

It all began in the heart of a lively college campus, where students hurried from lecture halls to libraries, their minds consumed with assignments and exams. Amid the rush of college life, there was one thing that never failed to bring people together—chai. And not just any chai, but the kind served at Chai Cinema Café, affectionately known as CCC. Nestled just a short walk away from campus, CCC wasn't just a café; it was a sanctuary for students seeking a break from their busy lives.

But there was a challenge. CCC was new. Students weren't yet familiar with its unique chai blends or its cozy corners where the best conversations unfolded. How could I make CCC more than just a café—it needed to become the destination, the place that students would crave during their free moments between classes.

Then, like a stroke of luck, the perfect opportunity came knocking: the college was hosting its annual freshers' event, a gathering of hundreds of eager first-years and their energetic seniors. It was the kind of event where connections were made, friendships blossomed, and most importantly—brands were born.

The college was offering sponsorships, and I immediately saw the potential for CCC. The price tag was ₹10,000 for a sponsorship, but I knew this was my chance to not just sponsor the event—but to make CCC the talk of the campus. I worked my charm and negotiated the deal down to ₹7,000, securing CCC a prime spot at the event. This wasn't just about putting CCC's name on a banner. No, this had to be bigger. CCC needed to feel like a part of every student's journey, their go-to spot for chai, snacks, and memories.

A Campaign Was Born

The idea was simple: create a campaign that wasn't just about visibility but about building a real connection with students. A campaign that would stick in their minds long after the freshers' event ended. And so, the CCC College Campaign was born—a multi-layered effort designed to make CCC the center of student life.

1. The Power of Humor: Catching Eyes with Banners

I knew the first step was to get students talking. The campus was full of bored lecture-goers, trudging from class to class, glued to their phones. I needed something that would catch their attention—and make them smile. That's where the banners came in.

I decided to infuse humor, the kind of humor that students would find familiar and fun. The banners, placed in high-traffic spots around campus, read like a conversation:

"Agar lecture nahi toh CCC ha sahi" — A lighthearted invitation to take a break at CCC, perfect for those moments when students found themselves free.

The banners did more than just catch attention—they sparked curiosity and conversations. Students started snapping pictures and sharing them on social media, tagging friends and joking about their shared love for skipping lectures in favor of a chai break. The humor struck a chord, turning CCC into a buzzword across the campus. It wasn't just an advertisement; it was a reflection of campus culture, a relatable nod to the little joys that made college life memorable. Slowly but surely, CCC was no longer just a name—it became an idea, a vibe, and a place students felt drawn to.

"Fresher ho ya purana, CCC ki chai banaye sabko deewana" — *A playful message for everyone, no matter if they were freshers or final-year students.*

This catchy message not only highlights the universal appeal of CCC's chai but also creates a sense of belonging for everyone on campus. By addressing both freshers and seniors, it bridges the gap between different batches, uniting them under the shared joy of enjoying chai at CCC. The lighthearted tone makes it approachable and memorable, ensuring that students see CCC as a welcoming space for all, regardless of where they are in their college journey.

"LPA ka sapna? Hamare chaiwale ki bhi 18 LPA!" — A cheeky jab at the high expectations students had for their future, suggesting that CCC was part of their aspirational world.

The reaction was immediate. Students didn't just see banners; they saw jokes that spoke to them. It was as if CCC had become a part of their day-to-day conversations. The next time someone mentioned chai, they couldn't help but mention CCC.

2. The Loyalty Program: Brewing Connections Over Time

But we didn't just want students to notice CCC once. We wanted them to return, to make CCC their regular hangout. That's when I introduced the 10th Meal Free loyalty program. For every nine meals purchased, students earned a free meal. The loyalty cards were distributed right at the freshers' event, and from that moment, students began collecting stamps like it was a treasure hunt. The best part? They felt special—like they were part of an exclusive club.

The loyalty program wasn't just about free meals—it was about forging a connection. Each visit became more than just a chai break; it was an opportunity to build a relationship with CCC. Students came back not just for the food but because CCC had become a part of their routine, a place they were loyal to.

3. Engaging the Crowd: Fun and Games on Stage

As a sponsor, we had the coveted stage time at the freshers' event. I decided to make the most of this moment by creating interactive games where students could win free meals at CCC. The crowd roared with excitement as participants took the stage, their energy infectious. These games weren't just about winning meals—they were about creating moments, experiences that students would remember long after the event ended. The winners, thrilled to claim their prize, often brought friends along. Each new visitor who walked into CCC felt like a part of a bigger story, and they brought others with them, spreading the buzz even further .The stage time became more than just a promotional opportunity—it transformed into a platform for connection. Students laughed, cheered, and bonded over the games, creating an electric atmosphere that resonated with the CCC brand. These moments turned CCC into more than just a café; it became synonymous with fun, friendship, and unforgettable memories. By the end of the event, CCC wasn't just in the minds of students—it was in their hearts, a place they couldn't wait to experience firsthand.

4. Social Media Magic: Spreading the Love Online

Of course, no campaign would be complete without tapping into the social media frenzy. Recognizing how crucial Instagram was for students, I launched an exclusive CCC Instagram filter for the event. The rules were simple: use the filter, post a story, tag CCC, and get a chance to win a free bun maska.

Thanks Sanika Chavan for being the face for filter

The result? The filter went viral. Students shared their stories, tagged their friends, and instantly CCC's presence spread across their feeds. The more students engaged online, the more they connected with CCC, even after the event had ended. The café wasn't just in their memories— it was in their Instagram stories too.

The Aftermath: CCC Becomes a Staple

Fast forward a year, and the results were clear. CCC wasn't just a café anymore—it had become the spot for students. The college crowd now made up 30% of CCC's overall revenue, and during pre-evening hours, students filled the café, chatting, laughing, and savoring their chai. The loyalty program had turned one-time visitors into regulars, and those banners? They'd become a part of campus folklore.

But the real success wasn't just in the numbers. It was in the stories. The stories of students who walked into CCC to study for exams, to celebrate birthdays, to catch up with friends. It was in the laughter echoing through the café, the memories being made with every sip of chai.

Lessons Learned: The Power of Relatability

Looking back, this campaign was more than just a marketing effort—it was about understanding the pulse of students, their humor, their dreams, their routines, and connecting with them on a personal level. It was about creating a brand that felt like part of their daily life, not just a place to get food.

CCC wasn't just a café anymore. It was a place where students felt at home, a place they would remember long after they'd graduated. And that, I realized, was the power of building a brand that speaks their language, meets them where they are, and becomes a part of their story.

me and my better quarter

Mad Over Pizza A Flavorful Launch with Local Flair in Pune

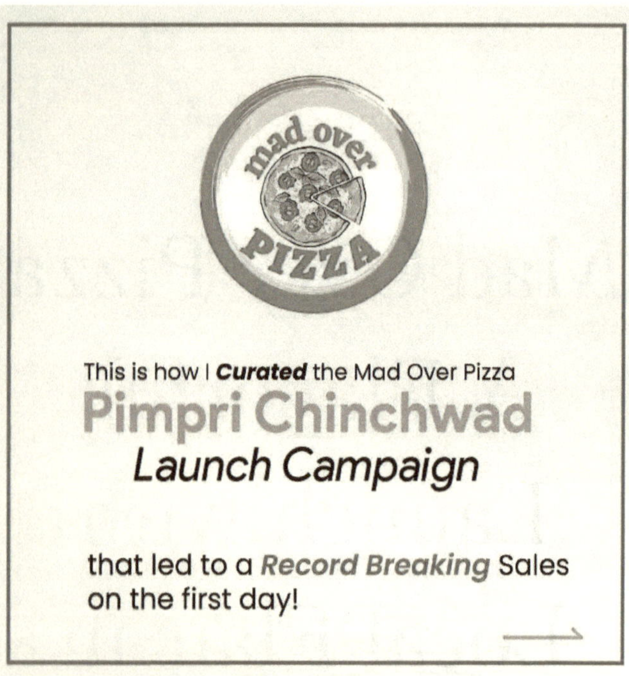

The Story of Mad Over Pizza's Grand Pune Debut

When the Mad Over Pizza (MOP) team decided to enter the bustling Pune market, the mission was clear—create an unforgettable first impression. Despite being a household name in other cities, Pune remained largely untouched by their tempting aromas and sizzling pizzas. The goal? To make sure MOP wasn't just another pizza chain to the people of Pune, but a brand that felt like home.

The Challenge: Creating a Local Connection

MOP's entry into Pune wasn't just about selling pizza—it was about embedding the brand into the fabric of local culture. The team needed to cut through the noise and capture the essence of Pune. The challenge was set: how to make MOP feel like a Pune resident's own, local favorite? To do this, the campaign would need to be bold, engaging, and culturally connected.

The Vision: A Celebration of Pune's Identity

The concept for the campaign began with a deep dive into Pune's heart and soul. Pune is a city rich in culture, language, and pride. MOP knew they had to leverage this by tapping into what made Pune, well, Pune. The strategy? A fun, vibrant campaign filled with humor, local symbols, and above all, language—the heart of any city's culture.

The tagline, "#MOP *ची स्वारी, पुण्याच्या दारी*," (MOP's march to Pune's doorstep) became the heartbeat of the campaign. It wasn't just about a brand arrival—it was about a celebration. This Marathi phrase evoked a sense of pride and excitement, allowing the people of Pune to feel like MOP was coming home.

A special thanks to Samyak Jain and Prasad Bhujbal for writing this tagline

Crafting the Campaign

The heart of the campaign was its ability to speak the language of Pune, both literally and figuratively. Every element—from design to content to strategy—was carefully crafted to resonate with the local audience.

Language: Everything, from social media posts to event promotions, was created in Marathi. By speaking the local language, the campaign immediately felt personal and approachable.

Design: Bright colors—reds, yellows, greens—were used to reflect the energy and vibrancy of Pune itself. The MOP mascot, a lovable character, became a familiar face in all the posts. Whether it was posing with quirky taglines or inviting locals to join in on the fun, the mascot bridged the gap between the brand and the community.

Multi-Channel Approach: The campaign wasn't just confined to one platform. It spanned social media, influencer partnerships, billboard advertisements, and even live events. The aim was to ensure no stone was left unturned in reaching the people of Pune.

The Execution: Making it Real

The excitement for MOP's arrival was palpable from the moment the campaign went live. A countdown began, with daily posts showcasing quirky phrases and vibrant visuals. As each day passed, the buzz around the launch only grew.

Influencer Collaboration: To amplify the campaign, MOP partnered with Hindavi Sarkar Patil, a local Instagram influencer with millions of followers. Hindavi's endorsement gave MOP instant credibility in Pune. Her posts, filled with excitement and humor, urged her followers to join the launch event and share in the celebration. Her involvement brought MOP into the local conversation, turning anticipation into action.

Billboards and Offline Marketing: Not forgetting the power of traditional marketing, MOP placed eye-catching billboards in high-traffic areas of Pimpri Chinchwad. These billboards weren't just informative—they were vibrant, with simple messages in Marathi, showcasing the launch date and exciting offers. The mascot's recognizable face was everywhere, making sure no one could forget MOP's impending arrival.

Launch Event: The grand event was designed to be more than just a store opening—it was a festival. Free cold coffee, live music, photo ops with the mascot, and engaging activities created an atmosphere of celebration. Locals, families, and foodies gathered not just to taste the pizza, but to be a part of a memorable experience.

The Impact: A City Transformed

The results? Nothing short of a success. Social media engagement surged with locals tagging friends, sharing posts, and creating their own content. The countdown posts, combined with Hindavi's influence, led to an outpouring of excitement online.

On launch day, the footfall at the Pimpri Chinchwad outlet was overwhelming. People flocked in, not only to try the pizza but to be a part of something they could proudly call their own. The live music, the free coffee, and the fun activities kept visitors engaged, and many shared their experiences online, giving MOP organic promotion in the process.

Key Takeaways

Cultural Relevance is Key: Speaking the local language and tapping into cultural pride proved to be the cornerstone of this campaign. MOP wasn't just another brand trying to sell a product—it was a brand that understood Pune.

Consistency Across Channels: The campaign was cohesive in every sense. From social media posts to billboards to the in-store experience, the visual language and messaging were consistent. This made the brand instantly recognizable.

Influencer Power: Partnering with local influencers helped MOP tap into an established community. Hindavi's genuine enthusiasm for the brand created an authentic connection with her followers.

The Magic of Multi-Channel Marketing: The blend of digital and traditional marketing ensured MOP reached a wide audience, from social media-savvy youth to those who prefer offline communication.

The Legacy: A Brand Born from Pune

As the dust settled and the launch event became a memory, one thing was clear—MOP had arrived in Pune, and it had arrived in style. Through strategic planning, a deep understanding of local culture, and a fun, engaging campaign, MOP didn't just enter Pune—it became a part of the city's vibrant landscape.

The campaign didn't just fill bellies—it filled hearts, creating loyal customers who saw MOP not as an outsider, but as a brand that spoke their language and understood their pride.

And as MOP's pizza ovens continue to churn out delicious pies, it's clear that the true recipe for success isn't just in the ingredients—it's in connecting with the people, creating experiences, and becoming part of the community.

A Pledge

I, Tabish Khan, pledge to contribute 25% of all profits generated from the sales of this book towards transforming lives through education for the underprivileged. This commitment stands as a step towards creating a brighter, more equitable future for those in need.

Why I wrote this?

The answer is simple: because I wanted to.